Persuasion

JANE AUSTEN

Level 2

Retold by Derek Strange
Series Editors: Andy Hopkins and Jocelyn Potter

Pearson Education Limited
Edinburgh Gate, Harlow,
Essex CM20 2JE, England
and Associated Companies throughout the world.

ISBN: 978-1-4058-6949-2

Persuasion was first published in 1818
This adaptation first published by Penguin Books 1991
Published by Addison Wesley Longman Ltd and Penguin Books Ltd 1998
This edition first published 2008

3 5 7 9 10 8 6 4 2

Text copyright © Derek Strange 1991
Illustrations copyright © David Cuzik 1991
This edition copyright © Pearson Education Ltd 2008

The moral right of the adapter and of the illustrator has been asserted

Typeset by Graphicraft Ltd, Hong Kong
Set in 11/14pt Bembo
Printed in China
SWTC/02

Published by Pearson Education Ltd in association with
Penguin Books Ltd, both companies being subsidiaries of Pearson Plc

For a complete list of the titles available in the Penguin Readers series please write to your local
Pearson Longman office or to: Penguin Readers Marketing Department, Pearson Education,
Edinburgh Gate, Harlow, Essex CM20 2JE, England.

Contents

Introduction

'I must be ready to hear the name Captain Wentworth at any time now,'
Anne thought sadly, 'and I must be ready to meet him again soon, too. I
must try to forget my love for him.'

Not many people are interested in Anne. She is the quiet second
daughter of Sir Walter Elliot and lives in Somersetshire with him
and her sister, Elizabeth. She has one good friend outside the
family, Lady Russell.

Years before, it was different. Then, Frederick Wentworth loved
her and she loved him. But Frederick went into the navy and his
ship carried him away...

Then, suddenly, Anne hears that he is coming back to
Somersetshire. He is going to visit his sister, and Anne is going
to meet him again. Now he is an important man, the captain of
a ship. Will he remember her? Does he love her now? Or must
Anne forget him again?

Jane Austen is one of the most important of all English writers.
She was born in 1775 in Hampshire in the south of England.
When she was a young woman, she lived, like Anne in this story,
in the city of Bath. She never married and never left the south of
England. She died quite young, in 1817.

She started writing when she was a child. She wrote some of
her most famous stories in her early twenties, but for many years
nobody outside her family read them. Her most famous books
are *Sense and Sensibility* (1811), *Pride and Prejudice* (1813), *Emma*
(1815) and *Persuasion* (1818). They are clever, funny love stories
about the people of her time – their parties and dinners, their
conversations and mistakes. Today, nearly two hundred years after
she wrote them, they are some of the most famous stories in the
English language.

Sir Walter Elliot lived at Kellynch Hall with two of his daughters,
Elizabeth and Anne.

Chapter 1   Kellynch

Sir Walter Elliot lived at Kellynch Hall, in Somersetshire, with two of his daughters, Elizabeth and Anne. His third daughter, Mary, did not live at the Hall. She met Mr Charles Musgrove; they married and Mary went away to live at Charles's home, in the village of Uppercross, not very far from Kellynch.

Sir Walter was fifty-four years old and was a handsome man. But he was not a clever man. He only thought about his hair and his moustache, or the colour of his coat or shirt or trousers. He never wanted to think about other things. His wife, Lady Elliot – a beautiful, clever and friendly woman – was now dead. The two girls stayed with their father at the Hall, but they often visited their mother's good friend, Lady Russell, and she often visited them.

Lady Russell lived in another big house, not far from Kellynch Hall. She loved her friend's three daughters very much, but she loved the second daughter, Anne, more than the other two. Anne was a pretty, but very quiet young woman. She was the cleverest of the three girls. She liked thinking; she liked talking to other people; she liked reading good books. But her father loved Elizabeth and Mary more than he loved Anne. He never talked about things with her. He wasn't interested in her. For Sir Walter, Anne was . . . Anne was only Anne.

Elizabeth looked after the Hall with its big gardens and beautiful park, and Anne helped her. Mary sometimes came to visit them.

Sir Walter, their father, never wanted to think about money. He liked buying new things for the house. He liked buying new jackets and shoes. He liked driving in expensive new carriages.

But he never asked, 'Where does the money come from? How much money have we got?' He did not like thinking about it.

So, after some years, the Elliot family didn't have much money. Sir Walter spoke to Elizabeth about it. Elizabeth spoke to Lady Russell about it. She asked Lady Russell to help them.

'What can we do?' she asked her mother's old friend.

'I do not know, but I can ask my friend Mr Shepherd,' Lady Russell answered. 'He is clever with money. He can help us.'

♦

Lady Russell came to the Hall with her friend, Mr Shepherd. They talked to Sir Walter and to Elizabeth.

'You must leave Kellynch Hall,' Mr Shepherd told them. 'This big house is too expensive for you. You must go and live in a smaller house.'

They all looked at Sir Walter. He was very quiet. He said nothing for a minute or two, but then he answered.

'Yes. You are right. We must leave Kellynch Hall and find a smaller house to live in. Perhaps we can look for a house in Bath. It is not very far from here, and I like living in Bath. It is a beautiful city. A lot of interesting, rich families live in Bath, you know!'

Anne listened. She was not happy. She did not like Bath – she remembered her three unhappy years at school there, after her mother died. But they didn't ask Anne. Sir Walter was not interested in Anne. They were going to leave her beautiful home, Kellynch Hall. Bath was going to be her new home.

♦

'You must leave Kellynch Hall. This house is too expensive for you.'

One day soon after this, Mr Shepherd was in Taunton, a town quite near Kellynch Hall. He met a man called Admiral Croft there, and his wife, Mrs Croft. The Crofts had no children and they were rich. Admiral Croft and his wife wanted to find a big house in Somersetshire, near Taunton.

'I am in the navy,' the Admiral told Mr Shepherd, 'but I have a holiday now for some months and I want to take a nice, quiet house near here for our holiday.'

Mr Shepherd told Admiral and Mrs Croft about Kellynch Hall. They were very interested. They wanted to see it.

'When can we visit Sir Walter Elliot and see his house, do you think, Mr Shepherd?' asked Mrs Croft.

Mr Shepherd asked Sir Walter the same question and the Crofts visited the Hall with Mr Shepherd one afternoon, a week later, for tea. They met Sir Walter, Elizabeth and Anne and they all sat together and had tea. The Admiral and his wife liked the house and its gardens very much – they asked many questions about it. Mr Shepherd wanted to know more about the Crofts too, so he asked them some questions.

'And, you know, Sir Walter,' Mr Shepherd said later, 'Mrs Croft comes from Somersetshire too. Her brother lives quite near Kellynch, she said. But what did she say her brother's name was, now? I cannot remember.'

Anne listened. She waited and then said quietly, 'Mr Wentworth is his name, I think.'

'That is the name! Mr Wentworth! Thank you, Miss Elliot.'

Anne stood up suddenly and walked quickly out, into the garden. She was excited; her face was hot and red and she did not want the other people in the room to see.

'In a few months, perhaps, *he* is going to be here ... at Kellynch!' she said quietly.

♦

Mrs Croft had two brothers. One of her brothers lived near Kellynch, in Somersetshire, but her second brother was a young officer in the navy. His name was Captain Frederick Wentworth.

Some years before, in the summer of 1806, the young Captain Wentworth came to stay with his older brother in Somersetshire. He was a very handsome, clever and strong young man. He met Anne, a pretty young nineteen-year-old girl, and the two young people soon fell in love.

They were very happy together, but only for a short time. Captain Wentworth spoke to Sir Walter one day.

The Crofts visited the Hall with Mr Shepherd one afternoon, for tea.

'Your daughter, Anne, and I are in love, sir,' he said. 'We are very happy together. I am here to ask you, Sir Walter, for your daughter's hand. We want to marry.'

Sir Walter did not say 'yes' or 'no'. He was cold and unfriendly to Captain Wentworth and he was not interested in his daughter, Anne. He did not want to help her to marry the young man she loved. He did not want Anne to be happy.

Lady Russell wanted Anne to be happy but she too did not want Anne to marry Captain Wentworth – she thought Anne was too young. Anne was only nineteen. And Captain Wentworth had no money. She wanted Anne to wait and find a richer, more important man to marry, not a young officer in the navy. Anne listened carefully to Lady Russell. The older woman's persuasion slowly began to work. Slowly, Anne started to think her love for Captain Wentworth was wrong.

'Perhaps I *am* too young,' she thought. 'And perhaps I cannot help Frederick to be happy. I must think of his work in the navy – perhaps he can do better without me. Perhaps Lady Russell is right – I know she loves me and is my friend.'

She saw Captain Wentworth one last time that summer. Her face was very sad. 'I am very sorry, Captain Wentworth,' she said to him, 'but I cannot marry you.'

'But we are happy together, Miss Elliot!' he answered. 'I do not understand this. Why. . . ?'

'I cannot say,' Anne answered, 'but that is my last word. We cannot marry.'

Captain Wentworth left Kellynch Hall that afternoon, and soon he left the country. He went to sea again in his ship.

Anne changed. She was quieter. Her pretty face was often sad. She loved Captain Wentworth. She was not going to marry Captain Wentworth, so now she did not want to marry anybody.

'I am here to ask you for your daughter's hand. We want to marry.'

For more than seven years, Captain Wentworth did not come back to England. He was now a rich man, and he was going to be in Somersetshire again – perhaps at Kellynch Hall, with his sister, Mrs Croft!

Chapter 2 Uppercross

Sir Walter and Elizabeth moved to live in a house in Bath early in September. Admiral and Mrs Croft were going to arrive to live at Kellynch Hall later that month.

Anne's younger sister, Mary, was ill, so Anne did not go to Bath with her father and her older sister in September. She went to Uppercross to stay with Mary and her husband, Charles, for some weeks. She was going to help Mary with her two young children.

Lady Russell drove Anne to Uppercross in her carriage.

Uppercross was a beautiful old English village, about three miles from Kellynch Hall. Charles's mother and father, Mr and Mrs Musgrove, and his two younger sisters lived in the biggest house in the village, and Charles and Mary lived in another smaller house near there, Uppercross Cottage.

Anne liked the Cottage, with its garden of flowers and fruit trees. Anne liked Mary's husband, Charles, too, and she liked Charles's two younger sisters, Henrietta and Louisa. They were pretty girls, nineteen and twenty years old. They liked dancing and singing and meeting new people. They were happy, friendly girls. And they liked Anne very much.

♦

On 29 September, Admiral and Mrs Croft arrived to live at Kellynch Hall. Soon after that, the Crofts came to visit the

Anne liked the Cottage, with its garden of flowers and fruit trees.

Musgroves in the big house and Mary and Anne at the Cottage one afternoon. Charles was not at home, but Mary sat and talked to the Admiral and Anne talked to Mrs Croft.

Suddenly, Anne heard the Admiral say to Mary, 'One of Mrs Croft's brothers is coming to stay with us soon at Kellynch Hall, you know.'

'Which of Mrs Croft's brothers is that?' asked Mary. 'I understand she has two.'

'Yes,' the Admiral started to answer, 'that is right. It is . . .'

But he did not finish his answer. Mary's two little boys wanted him to go and play, and they pulled him away to another corner of the room.

◆

Mr and Mrs Musgrove came to have dinner at Uppercross Cottage that evening, with Henrietta and Louisa. Henrietta came with her mother and father in their carriage, but Louisa wanted to walk to the Cottage through the park, and she arrived at the Cottage first.

'Mrs Croft's brother, Captain Wentworth, is back from sea and Mrs Croft says he is coming to stay with them soon at Kellynch Hall,' said Louisa, excitedly. 'Did the Crofts tell you that when they were here this afternoon? Mother says he is a very handsome young man – he was here in Somersetshire seven or eight years ago, she says, and he is now an officer in the navy!'

Some minutes later, Mr and Mrs Musgrove arrived with Henrietta, and they all talked for some time about the visit of Captain Wentworth to his sister at Kellynch Hall.

'I must be ready to hear the name of Captain Wentworth at any time now,' Anne thought sadly, 'and I must be ready to meet him again soon, too. I must try to forget my love for him.'

◆

Three or four days after this, Captain Wentworth arrived at Kellynch Hall. Mr and Mrs Musgrove invited him and the Crofts to come to dinner with them at Uppercross a week later.

Charles and Mary went to the big house for dinner, too. Anne stayed with their two children at the Cottage. So Charles and Mary met Captain Wentworth for the first time. Charles invited him to visit them the next day at the Cottage and so it was there that Captain Wentworth and Anne met again after more than seven years.

She heard his voice outside the door, he came in, her eyes met his, he gave a small polite smile; the other people in the room –

He came in, her eyes met his, he gave a small polite smile.

Mary, Henrietta, Louisa – all wanted to talk to him. Charles came in and said something to him and then the two men left.

Henrietta and Louisa left a minute or two after them, and Anne tried to listen to Mary. She tried, but she heard nothing. The only words in her head were 'He was here! He was here! In this room!'

From that day, Captain Wentworth and Anne were often together in the same room. He never talked much to Anne but she listened to him often with the other people in the house. He talked a lot to Henrietta and Louisa – they often sat next to him and they asked him about the navy and about his visits to other countries. They liked listening to his stories of the sea. He was a very handsome man and, after some days, Anne saw, the two young girls were in love with him. They laughed a lot together and he was happy to be with them. With Anne, he was always quiet and polite, but he was not warm or friendly and he never laughed with her.

♦

Soon, Captain Wentworth was at Uppercross four or five times a week. One morning, he came into the sitting-room of the Cottage, and found only Anne there with one of Mary's children. The child was ill. Usually, other people were in the room with him and Anne, but that morning only Anne and the child were there.

'Oh, I am sorry, Miss Elliot,' he said. He stopped near the door. 'I thought the two Miss Musgroves were here.'

Then he walked quickly to the window and looked out. He had nothing more to say to her.

'They are coming in a minute, I think,' said Anne.

She wanted to stand up and run out of the room. She did not want Frederick to be polite and cold to her!

12

He talked a lot to Henrietta and Louisa. They liked listening to his stories of the sea.

'But I must stay in the room and talk to him,' she thought. 'What can I say to him? And what can he say to me?'

Suddenly, Mary's younger child, Walter, ran into the room and jumped up on Anne's back.

'Carry me! Carry me, please!' the child sang.

'No, Walter. I do not want to play with you now. Please get down. You are heavy.'

The child did not move. He did not want to get down. He wanted a game. He stayed on her back.

'Walter, please . . . !' Anne tried again.

But the child did not move.

Suddenly, Captain Wentworth walked across the room from the window, took the child off her back and carried him away.

She was amazed. She forgot to thank him – no words came.

'He helped me!' Anne thought. 'Why? He watched me and he came to help me.'

Captain Wentworth sat in another corner of the room with the child and played with him. Then luckily Mary and Henrietta and Louisa came into the room and Anne left quickly.

It was a small, unimportant thing, but Anne wanted to think about it.

♦

It was autumn. The trees were brown and yellow in the park of the big house at Uppercross.

For the next week or two, Anne was often with Captain Wentworth and Henrietta and Louisa Musgrove. They walked in the park or along the small roads to other villages near Uppercross. Anne watched and listened but she thought Captain Wentworth

14

Captain Wentworth walked across the room, took the child off her back and carried him away.

was not in love with Henrietta or Louisa. He liked them, but he was not in love with them, she thought.

One afternoon, because the weather was warm and sunny, they went for a longer walk than they usually did. They were not far from Kellynch Hall. They were all quite tired, so they stopped and sat down under a big tree for some minutes. Suddenly, they saw Admiral Croft and his wife in their small carriage in the little road near them. Mrs Croft saw them and the Admiral stopped his carriage.

'You have a very long walk back to Uppercross and it is quite late,' said the Admiral. 'Can we take one of you with us? We can easily take one more in the carriage, you know.'

Henrietta and Louisa were not very tired, so they said 'No, thank you.' Mary said 'no', too.

Mrs Croft turned to Anne and said, '*You* are tired, Miss Elliot. I can see. You must come with us in the carriage. We can very easily take you.'

Anne smiled and was going to say 'No, thank you' but Captain Wentworth turned and looked at her quietly. Then, without a word, he took her arm and helped her up into the Crofts' little carriage.

Again, Anne was amazed, and again she forgot to thank him.

'He saw I was tired, so he put me here!' she thought.

The Admiral drove off along the road to Uppercross with his wife and Anne. Anne talked and answered their questions without thinking, but then they began to talk about 'Frederick' and Anne listened.

'I think it is time he found a wife now,' said the Admiral. 'He likes those two Musgrove girls, but the question is which of the two?'

'Yes, which? They are very pretty girls, but I do not think he is

Without a word, he took her arm and helped her up into the Crofts'
little carriage.

in love with them and it is not easy to say which he likes most,'
answered his wife.

Chapter 3   Lyme

For two or three days after the long walk and the drive in the
carriage with the Crofts, Anne did not see Captain Wentworth at
Uppercross. He was away. He went to visit his old friend Captain
Harville in the town of Lyme, by the sea, seventeen miles from
Uppercross. When he came back, he told them about the beautiful
small town of Lyme.

It was November now, but the weather was quite warm.
Captain Wentworth talked about going back to Lyme for some
days to be with his friends there. The other young people at
Uppercross all wanted to go too. Louisa was the most excited
about going to Lyme. She asked her mother and father about it
and they said 'yes'.

They went in two carriages. The four young women – Mary,
Anne, Henrietta and Louisa – went in a big carriage, and Charles
and Captain Wentworth drove in a smaller carriage, behind them.
The two carriages arrived in Lyme after twelve o'clock, so there
was not much time to see the town that afternoon. They went first
to find rooms in a small hotel. They asked for their dinner to be
ready at seven o'clock, then they all walked down to the sea
together.

They walked past Captain Harville's house, near the beach, and
Captain Wentworth went inside to say 'hello' to his friends there.
The others went down to the beach. There was a long sea wall
there, called 'The Cobb', and they walked out along it. Soon, they
saw Captain Wentworth with three friends, on the beach, coming
to meet them. Captain Wentworth was with Captain Harville and

his wife, and another young officer in the navy, Captain Benwick. They all met on The Cobb and walked back to the Harvilles' house together.

Anne and Henrietta were the first people to be up early the next morning, so they went for a short walk down to the sea together before breakfast. The wind from the sea was cold in the early morning but it was another beautiful November day. After some time, they turned to go back to the hotel, and there on the beach they saw Captain Wentworth. They all walked back to the hotel together.

At the door of the hotel, they met another gentleman, coming out. His carriage waited by the door. They didn't know him. He was about thirty years old – not handsome, but he had a nice face. He moved back quickly and opened the hotel door for them very politely.

'Thank you, sir,' said Anne. She looked at the polite gentleman and she saw in his eyes that he thought she was beautiful.

Anne was very pretty that morning, after her walk in the early morning by the sea. Captain Wentworth saw the quick look in the polite gentleman's eyes, too, and he looked more carefully at Anne.

His eyes suddenly seemed to say 'Yes, you are beautiful this morning. This is the same Anne Elliot I knew and loved more than seven years ago.'

At breakfast, Captain Wentworth asked one of the people in the hotel about the gentleman at the door.

'Can you tell us his name?'

'Yes, sir,' the man answered. 'That is a Mr William Elliot. A very rich gentleman, sir. He arrived by ship last night, from Sidmouth. He's going from here to Bath, and then to London, I think, sir.'

'William Elliot!' said Mary. 'That must be our cousin, Anne!

And here in the same hotel with us! He is going to be the next head of the Elliot family, when father dies, you know, Captain Wentworth.'

'I am happy to know that the next head of the family is a gentleman . . .' Anne said, but she left her words unfinished because Captain and Mrs Harville and Captain Benwick arrived and took them for a walk in Lyme.

◆

They walked first through the streets of the old town. Then Louisa said she wanted to walk along The Cobb again, so they all went back to the beach. The Harvilles did not come with them – Captain Harville had a bad leg and he was tired, so they stopped at their house. Captain Benwick walked on with them to The Cobb.

The wind was quite strong on the sea wall, so they all went down to the beach below it. Louisa wanted to jump down from the wall and Captain Wentworth gave her his hand to help her. She smiled and jumped, but she did not catch his hand and she fell. Her head hit the beach, hard. She did not move. They all stood, without speaking.

Then Henrietta started to cry, 'Louisa! Louisa!'

'She is dead!' said Mary, her face white.

Captain Wentworth took Louisa's head in his arms. His face was as white as Louisa's. Charles and Anne took Henrietta's arms and helped her to sit down before she, too, fell.

'Somebody help me, please,' said Captain Wentworth.

'Help him! Help him!' said Anne. 'Leave me. I can easily look after Henrietta. Help Captain Wentworth with Louisa, quickly.'

Captain Benwick and Charles moved quickly to help Captain Wentworth.

Captain Wentworth took Louisa's head in his arms.

'A doctor,' said Anne. 'We must get a doctor.'

'That is right. A doctor,' Captain Wentworth said.

'I know where the doctor lives,' said Captain Benwick, and he started to walk quickly along The Cobb to the beach and to the town.

'What can we do for her, Anne?' Charles asked.

Captain Wentworth turned to Anne for help, too.

'We must carry her to the hotel, slowly and carefully,' said Anne.

They started to carry Louisa slowly along the sea wall. When they were outside the Harville's little house, the door opened and Captain and Mrs Harville came out quickly to help them.

'You must bring her in here. The doctor can come here to see her,' Captain Harville said.

They put Louisa into Mrs Harville's bed and the doctor soon arrived. He looked carefully at the cut on Louisa's head.

'No, she is not dead. But this is a very bad cut,' the doctor said. 'She must stay in bed for two or three weeks. She must not move from her bed.'

So Louisa stayed with the Harvilles at their little house in Lyme and Charles stayed at the hotel in the town – he wanted to be near his sister and to help Mrs Harville with her.

The others went back sadly to Uppercross in the carriage.

♦

Anne had only two more days at Uppercross. Two days later, Lady Russell came to take her to Sir Walter and Elizabeth's new house in Bath.

It was a dark day with rain in the sky when Anne drove away from Uppercross with Lady Russell, to Bath. They knew, from one

They put Louisa into Mrs Harville's bed and the doctor soon arrived.

of Elizabeth's letters to Lady Russell, that Mr Elliot, the gentleman at the hotel in Lyme, was now in Bath.

'And I hear he is a very handsome young man, Anne,' said Lady Russell. 'It is going to be very interesting to meet the next head of the Elliot family, I think.'

Anne did not say a word.

Chapter 4   Bath

Sir Walter's house in Bath was in Camden-place, one of the best streets in the city. Many rich and important families lived in Camden-place, so Sir Walter and Elizabeth were happy.

Anne's father and sister were happy to see her and show her their new house. They told her about their new friends in Bath, about the people they did or did not want to know in Bath, about the teashops and other good shops in Bath. They did not ask about Uppercross or Kellynch. They were only interested in Bath. Anne listened politely.

'And our cousin, Mr Elliot, came to see us too, Anne,' said Elizabeth happily. 'He arrived in Bath some days ago and called to see us. Father did not much like him when he was a younger man, but now he is a nice, handsome young gentleman, and Father likes him very much. He is staying in Bath for the winter, too.'

'He came to visit us four or five times last week,' said Sir Walter. 'Had dinner with us last Thursday. A very polite young man.'

Anne listened to all this.

'Why does Mr Elliot suddenly want to know my father and my sister?' she thought. 'Why is he suddenly interested in us after all this time? Perhaps it is Elizabeth he is interested in, and not Father.'

All through dinner they talked about Mr Elliot, and suddenly, after dinner, Mr Elliot arrived to visit them. When he came into the room, he was amazed to see Anne there, but very happy to meet her again.

'Miss Anne Elliot! My cousin! And we were in the same hotel together in Lyme! I am very happy to know your name this time,' he said.

He sat down with them and they talked about Lyme and the hotel there and Anne told him about Louisa's accident. He stayed for an hour. He liked sitting and talking to Anne – the time went very quickly!

◆

24

*Anne's father and sister were happy to see her and show her
their new house.*

The winter weeks went by, and Anne got to know Mr Elliot better and better. She did not understand why he was suddenly interested in them after ten years without knowing them, but she slowly started to like him. He was always friendly and polite to her – sometimes too friendly and too polite perhaps, she thought.

Her friend, Lady Russell, liked Mr Elliot. She thought he was interested in Anne and was perhaps in love with her. Perhaps he was the rich and important husband Lady Russell wanted to find for Anne? Anne did not think this. She told Lady Russell one day that she was not interested in marrying Mr Elliot.

Anne also met an old school friend, called Mrs Smith, and started to visit her quite often. Mrs Smith was ill and did not go out much – she had no money. Her husband was dead and she lived very quietly in two small rooms not far from Camden-place. Anne always liked visiting Mrs Smith. Lady Russell often took her to Mrs Smith's house in her carriage, and then Anne sat and talked to her friend all morning. Mrs Smith was a clever woman and was always happy and friendly – she never talked about her illness to Anne.

◆

February came. One day, a thick letter came from Mary in Uppercross, too. It came to Bath with Admiral and Mrs Croft. They were in Bath for some weeks because the Admiral wanted to see a doctor there, and to visit some old friends from the navy.

Mary's letter told Anne that Louisa was better after her accident, but that she was in Lyme with the Harvilles. Louisa and the young Captain Benwick were in love, Mary said, and Captain Benwick wanted to marry her.

Mr Elliot was always friendly and polite to her — sometimes too friendly and polite perhaps.

'So Louisa is not going to marry Captain Wentworth, you see.'

'So Louisa is not going to marry Captain Wentworth, you see. And we all thought that Captain Benwick was in love with you *when we were in Lyme, but we were wrong,'* Mary wrote.

Anne was very happy for Captain Benwick and Louisa. She was also happy to know that the Crofts were in Bath now... and to know that Captain Wentworth was not going to marry Louisa.

The Crofts came to visit them and Anne often saw the Admiral and his wife walking in the town. She saw that they were always very happy when they were together. One day, after a visit to her friend Mrs Smith, Anne met the Admiral in the street outside. The Admiral walked back to Camden-place with Anne and they talked about Captain Benwick and Louisa.

Suddenly the Admiral said 'All this is quite unlucky for Frederick, you know. My wife and I thought Miss Musgrove was in love with him, but she was not. We are thinking of inviting him to come and stay with us here in Bath. Do you not think, Miss Elliot,' the Admiral asked, 'that we must get young Frederick to Bath?'

♦

The next time Anne went out into the town, she saw Captain Wentworth. She was in a small teashop, near the window, when suddenly Captain Wentworth walked in with some of his friends. He saw her and his face went quite red: she saw in his eyes that he was at the same time amazed and sad, but perhaps happy to see her again. He spoke to her and then turned quickly away and spoke to one of his friends, but he was not cold and he was not friendly to her. After a minute or two, he turned to her again.

'You are going home, I see, Miss Elliot, but it is raining and you have no coat. Can I help you to find a carriage? You cannot walk home in the rain.'

'Thank you, Captain Wentworth, but no. I am going with Mr Elliot, my cousin. He is walking home with me. Ah, here is Mr Elliot now.'

Captain Wentworth remembered Mr Elliot very well: the man outside the hotel in Lyme, looking at Anne in the early morning and thinking she was beautiful. Mr Elliot came in quickly, and because of the rain, he wanted to leave the teashop quickly, before it rained harder. She only had time quickly to say 'Good morning to you' to Captain Wentworth, before she was out in the street, walking home with her hand under Mr Elliot's arm. But many questions about Captain Wentworth danced in her head! Was he unhappy about Louisa's marriage to Captain Benwick? Was he happy to see her in the teashop? How long was he going to stay in Bath with his sister?

Nothing happened for a day or two, then an important friend of Sir Walter invited all the Elliots to go to the theatre one evening.

They arrived early at the theatre and waited by one of the fires inside. Suddenly, the door opened and Captain Wentworth came in. Anne was nearest to him.

'How do you do?' she asked when he saw her. He stopped and they talked for a minute or two about the weather in Bath and about the Crofts. Then they had nothing more to say, but he did not leave her. Suddenly, he started to speak again – about Louisa's accident and her love for Captain Benwick. 'He wants me to understand that he was not in love with Louisa at Uppercross and in Lyme,' she thought. 'Is he trying to tell me that he loves me?' she thought.

When they went into the theatre, Anne walked without seeing anything, without hearing anything; she was very, very happy. Mr Elliot sat next to her, but it was difficult to listen to him, to talk to him, to think. Captain Wentworth was with his friends, quite near them, and she knew that he watched her with Mr Elliot – she saw his face change when he saw them together. He did not like to see her with her cousin, the polite Mr Elliot. For a minute she was happy that he did not like it. She knew now that he loved her after all this time, but then she thought 'I must show Frederick that I do not like this cousin, this Mr Elliot, that he is nothing to me. But how can I tell him?'

◆

'Is he trying to tell me that he loves me?' she thought.

The next afternoon, Anne went again to see her friend, Mrs Smith. She wanted to tell her all about the evening at the theatre. She knew her friend liked to hear everything.

'I know you had a very good evening, Anne,' said Mrs Smith. 'I can see in your eyes that you are happy today, that last night you were with the man you love more than all the world.'

Anne's face went red. How did Mrs Smith know about Captain Wentworth?

'But, please tell me, Anne,' Mrs Smith went on, 'does Mr Elliot know about me? Does he know that I am in Bath?'

'Mr Elliot?' Anne asked. 'Do you know Mr Elliot?'

She suddenly saw Mrs Smith's mistake: her friend thought that Anne was in love with Mr Elliot.

'Yes, I know William Elliot very, very well,' Mrs Smith said quietly and sadly. 'And I can see that you are in love with him, that perhaps you are going to marry him.'

'Marry Mr Elliot?' Anne was amazed. 'I am not going to marry Mr Elliot! It is not Mr Elliot that I . . .' She stopped. 'Why did you think that?' she asked.

'Because I know you are often together, and I know some of your friends here think the same thing too.' She suddenly smiled again. 'But I am very happy to hear that you are not in love with Mr Elliot and that you are not going to marry him.'

'Why are you happy about it?' Anne asked, and so Mrs Smith told her about Mr Elliot.

'He is a cold, dark man,' she said. She was angry now. 'When I was young, before my husband died, Mr Elliot was my husband's best friend. My husband loved him – I know that he often helped Mr Elliot with money. Mr Elliot always wanted money. He only wanted to be rich, so he married a girl from a rich family. But he did not love her – her money was all he wanted. When Mr Elliot had a lot of money, he turned away from my husband; he didn't want to know him. When my husband was ill and when he died, he left me with no money. Mr Elliot did not want to help me or hear about me. Then last year, his wife died too, and he had all her money. The next thing he wanted was to have an important name, to be "Sir William Elliot", the head of the Elliot family. So he came back to Somersetshire, to Bath, and tried to get to know your father and sister again. He is only interested in William Elliot. He is never interested in other people. He is a very bad man.'

Anne listened to Mrs Smith's story and she read some

Her friend's story was all true. Mr Elliot was a very bad man.

letters from Mr Elliot to her friend and to her dead husband. She saw that her friend's story was all true. Mr Elliot was a very bad man.

♦

She went home. She was happy that Mr Elliot was away from Bath for a day or two – there were a lot of things to think about, and she must tell Lady Russell the story about him. She must ask Lady Russell to help her. But when she arrived back at Camden-place, she had no time to think. She found that Charles and Mary were there – they were in Bath for ten days.

Elizabeth talked about giving a big dinner for them, with some of their new friends in Bath, the next day. She sat down and wrote letters inviting people to come to the dinner and she invited Captain Wentworth to come too, 'because he is one of Charles's friends,' she said.

The next morning, Anne went to visit Mary at the hotel she and Charles were in. Other people were there too. Captain Wentworth was there, at a desk in one corner of the room, writing a letter. He finished and stood up, ready to leave. Suddenly he pushed the letter across the desk in front of Anne's eyes and then quickly left the room. The letter was to 'Miss A. E. –'. Anne fell into a chair near the desk, opened the letter and read:

'I must speak. I cannot go on without knowing. My love for you is not dead – I cannot love anybody but you. Why do you think I am here in Bath? For you. What do I think about all day? You. You must see that I am waiting for you – after eight and a half years now, I am here waiting for you. Please do not tell me that I am too late. F.W.'

Captain Wentworth was there, at a desk in one corner of the
room, writing a letter.

They talked about the love they now knew they had.

Anne did not move or speak. She was white. The others saw her white face. 'You are ill, Anne,' said Charles. 'I must find a carriage and take you home to Camden-place,' but Anne did not want to go in a carriage. She wanted to walk. She wanted to try to see Captain Wentworth in the street, to answer his letter with a word or a look. She wanted him to know, now, that she loved him, too.

They were in Union-street when they saw him. He turned and saw them when Charles called to him 'Captain Wentworth!' He stopped and came across the street. He did not look at Anne.

'Are you going up to Camden-place, perhaps?' Charles asked. 'Can you walk with Miss Elliot? She was not well at our hotel and now I am taking her home for an hour or two before the dinner this evening. But I must be at the gunshop in the market square in ten minutes. The man there wants to show me a new gun. Perhaps you can take my place and walk with Miss Elliot?'

Captain Wentworth smiled, said 'yes', and in half a minute Charles turned and left them. They started to walk slowly up the street together, Anne with her hand under Captain Wentworth's arm. They began to talk. After another minute, they turned together into a little garden, and sat there together to talk about the sad story of the past eight and a half years. And in all the years after that morning, they never forgot what happened in that garden and the things they said. They talked about the past four or five months, of Uppercross, of Henrietta and Louisa, of their days in Lyme and of the love they now knew they had.

By the time Anne and Captain Wentworth arrived back at Camden-place, they were two of the happiest people in the world.

♦

Anne and Captain Wentworth were to be married in the spring.

When Mr Elliot heard this, he soon left Bath – he did not want to marry Elizabeth, and he knew that Anne knew his story from her friend, Mrs Smith. Lady Russell, too, started to like Captain Wentworth. She wanted most to see Anne happy. She saw now that Captain Wentworth loved Anne and that Anne loved him – that all Anne wanted in the world was to be the wife of this handsome young officer.

ACTIVITIES

Chapter 1

Before you read

1 Look at the pictures in this book. What do you think the story is about?

    a detectives **b** children **c** the sea **d** love **e** sport

2 Read the Word List at the back of the book. Then discuss these questions.

    a When do you use persuasion with your friends?

    b Would you like to be an officer in the navy? Why (not)?

    c Were people more polite in Jane Austen's time?

While you read

3 Write the names.

    a He is Anne's father.   ....

    b She is Charles Musgrove's wife.   ....

    c She was a friend of Anne's dead mother. ....

    d She is the wife of an admiral.   ....

    e He is Mrs Croft's younger brother.   ....

    f She doesn't want to marry anybody. ....

After you read

4 Why are these places important to the story?

    a Kellynch Hall **b** Bath

5 Who says these words? Who or what is the speaker talking about?

    a 'He is clever with money. He can help us.'

    b 'In a few months, perhaps, *he* is going to be here.'

    c 'We cannot marry.'

6 Work with another student. Have the conversation, seven years ago, between Anne and Lady Russell. Talk about Captain Wentworth. Will he be a good husband for Anne?

Chapter 2

Before you read

7 In this chapter, Anne and Captain Wentworth meet again after many years. Discuss these questions.

    a Your friend goes away for many years. When they come back, are they the same person? Can you be friends in the same way as before?

    b What will happen between Anne and Captain Wentworth?

While you read

8 What happens first? What happens next? Write the numbers 1–6.

    a Admiral and Mrs Croft move to Kellynch Hall. .....

    b Captain Wentworth helps Anne with Mary's son Walter. .....

    c Anne goes to Uppercross and stays with her sister Mary. .....

    d Admiral and Mrs Croft talk about a wife for Captain Wentworth. .....

    e Anne sees Captain Wentworth for the first time in many years. .....

    f Captain Wentworth is friendly with Henrietta and Louisa Musgrove. .....

After you read

9 Are these sentences right or wrong?

    a Anne likes Henrietta and Louisa.

    b Captain Wentworth is warm and friendly with Anne.

    c He laughs with Henrietta and Louisa but not with Anne.

    d Anne and Captain Wentworth talk about their past love.

    e Anne thinks Captain Wentworth is handsome and kind.

10 Will Captain Wentworth marry one of the Musgrove sisters? Why (not)?

Chapter 3

Before you read

11 In this chapter, Anne and her friends visit a town by the sea. What do you think people did by the sea in Jane Austen's time?

While you read

12 Write the names in the sentences.

Louisa   Mrs Harville   Anne   William Elliot   Captain Benwick
Charles

a .... and her husband live at Lyme.

b Captain Wentworth knew .... in the navy.

c .... is staying at the same hotel as Anne, but Anne doesn't know him.

d .... has an accident on the beach.

e .... stays at the hotel after the other people go home.

f .... is going to meet her cousin in Bath.

After you read

13 When Louisa has her accident, who does what?

a Captain Wentworth	gets a doctor.
b Charles and Anne	puts his arms round Louisa.
c Benwick and Charles	take Louisa into their house.
d Captain Benwick	says, 'She is dead!'
e The Harvilles	help Henrietta.
f Mary	help Wentworth with Louisa.

14 What do we know about Mr William Elliot? Why is he important to Anne and her sisters?

15 Work with a friend. Discuss these questions.

a Would you like to visit Lyme?

b Do you do the same things as Anne and her friends when you are by the sea?

Chapter 4, pages 23–31

Before you read

16 Discuss these questions about the next chapter.

    a Which of these places will Anne visit in Bath?

        her father's home   her friend's home

        the train station   the doctor's   the theatre

    b Anne is going to meet her cousin, Mr Elliot. Will she like him?

    c Two people are going to marry. Who?

While you read

17 Which are the right words in *italics*?

    a Sir Walter and Elizabeth *like / don't like* Bath.

    b They talk about *Mr Elliot / Admiral Croft*.

    c Anne *likes / doesn't like* Mr Elliot.

    d Anne *wants / doesn't want* to marry Mr Elliot.

    e Anne's friend, Mrs Smith, is *rich / not rich*.

    f Louisa is going to marry *Captain Wentworth / Captain Benwick.*

    g Captain Wentworth is *happy / sad* about Louisa.

    h Captain Wentworth *likes / doesn't like* seeing Anne with her cousin.

After you read

18 Who says these words? Who or what is the speaker talking about?

    a 'Why is he suddenly interested in us after all this time?'

    b 'We all thought that Captain Benwick was in love with *you* when we were in Lyme, but we were wrong.'

    c 'I must show Frederick . . . that he is nothing to me.'

19 Work with a friend. You are Anne and Lady Russell. Talk about Mr Elliot. Is he a better man than Captain Wentworth?

Chapter 4, pages 32–38

Before you read

20 Discuss these questions.

    a In these pages, we learn more things about Mr Elliot. Will they be good or bad things?

    b How will the story end? Which of these people will <u>not</u> be happy?

    Anne Elliot   Mr Elliot   Lady Russell

    Captain Wentworth   Admiral and Mrs Croft

While you read

21 What happens first? What happens next? Write the numbers 1–6.

    a Mrs Smith thinks that Anne loves Mr Elliot.   .....

    b Anne and Captain Wentworth sit in a garden and talk.   .....

    c Mrs Smith tells Anne about her husband's best friend.   .....

    d Captain Wentworth gives Anne a letter.   .....

    e Charles and Mary arrive in Bath.   .....

    f Charles thinks that Anne is ill.   .....

After you read

22 Are these sentences right or wrong?

    a Mr Elliot gave Mrs Smith's husband a lot of money.

    b Captain Wentworth loved Anne all the time when he was away from her.

    c Captain Wentworth and Anne are going to marry.

    d Mr Elliot wants to marry Elizabeth.

    e Lady Russell is angry about Anne and Captain Wentworth.

23 Work with another student and have this conversation.

    Student A: You are Anne. Tell Mrs Smith about your plans for a life with Captain Wentworth.

    Student B: You are Mrs Smith. Ask about Anne's love for Captain Wentworth.

Writing

24 You are writing *Persuasion* for television or radio. Write the conversation between Anne and Captain Wentworth in the little garden (See page 37).

25 You are Anne. Write a letter to Lady Russell. Tell her about Louisa's accident at Lyme.

26 You are Mr Elliot, Lady Russell or Mrs Smith. Write about Anne's plans for a life with Captain Wentworth. How do you feel about them?

27 Write about Anne. Do you like her? Why (not)?

28 Write a short 'word picture' of one of these people: Sir Walter Elliot, Mr Elliot, Louisa Musgrove. Use the story and the pictures in this book.

29 You live in Jane Austen's time. You are writing a book about interesting cities in Europe. Write about Bath. What can visitors do there?

30 Would you like to live in Jane Austen's time? Why (not)?

31 Write a note to a friend about this book. Did you like it? Will your friend like it? Why (not)?

WORD LIST *with example sentences*

admiral (n) The *admiral's* ship was in front, with forty ships behind him.

ago (adv) He is twenty-one. He left school four years *ago*.

amazed (adj) She's usually very quiet. So we were *amazed* when she started shouting.

captain (n) The *captain* of the ship spoke to his men.

carriage (n) They drove home in a two-horse *carriage*.

corner (n) There were chairs in all four *corners* of the room.

cottage (n) The village had one big house and about thirty *cottages*.

cousin (n) The children of your uncles and aunts are your *cousins*.

far (adj/adv) It isn't *far* from here – only half a kilometre.

gentleman (n) Her first husband had to work for his money, but her second husband was a *gentleman*.

handsome (adj) He was a very *handsome* young man, and girls couldn't stop looking at him.

Lady (n) Before she married an important man, *Lady* Branson's name was Miss Smith.

must (v) 'He doesn't love me. I *must* try to forget him.' she thought.

navy (n) He liked ships and the sea. So he went into the *navy* when he left school.

officer (n) The captain and two other *officers* were on the ship.

persuasion (n) My mother's *persuasion* changed my ideas and plans.

polite (adj) *Polite* people say 'please' and 'thank you'.

soon (adv) It's January 29th today, so it'll be February *soon*.

together (adj/adv) The two friends often sit *together*.

true (adj) He says he's eighteen. Is that *true*, or is he only sixteen?

A Christmas Carol
Charles Dickens

Scrooge is a cold, hard man. He loves money, and he doesn't like people. He really doesn't like Christmas. But then some ghosts visit him. They show him his past life, his life now, and a possible future. Will Scrooge learn from the ghosts? Can he change?

The Prince and the Pauper
Mark Twain

Two babies are born on the same day in England. One boy is a prince and the other boy is from a very poor family. Ten years later, they change places for a game. But then the old king dies and they cannot change back. Will the poor boy be the new King of England?

Alice in Wonderland
Lewis Carroll

One hot summer day, Alice sees a white rabbit and runs after it. She follows it down a rabbit-hole – and arrives in 'Wonderland'. Here, caterpillars can talk and rabbits have watches. And the Queen wants to cut off everybody's head!

There are hundreds of Penguin Readers to choose from – world classics, film adaptations, modern-day crime and adventure, short stories, biographies, American classics, non-fiction, plays ...

For a complete list of all Penguin Readers titles, please contact your local Pearson Longman office or visit our website.

www.penguinreaders.com

PENGUIN READERS *recommends*

Black Beauty
Anna Sewell

'Always be good, so people will love you. Always work hard and do your best.'

These were the words of Black Beauty's mother to her son when they lived with Farmer Grey. But when Black Beauty grew up and his life changed, this was sometimes very difficult for him. Not everybody was as kind as Farmer Grey.

Treasure Island
Robert Louis Stevenson

A young boy, Jim Hawkins, lives quietly by the sea with his mother and father. One day, Billy Bones comes to lives with them and from that day everything is different. Jim meets Long Jim Silver, a man with one leg, and Jim and Long John Silver go far across the sea in a ship called the *Hispaniola* to Treasure Island.

Moby Dick
Herman Melville

Moby Dick is the most dangerous whale in the oceans. Captain Ahab fought him and lost a leg. Now he hates Moby Dick. He wants to kill him. But can Captain Ahab and his men find the great white whale? A young sailor, Ishmael, tells the story of their exciting and dangerous trip.

There are hundreds of Penguin Readers to choose from – world classics, film adaptations, modern-day crime and adventure, short stories, biographies, American classics, non-fiction, plays ...

For a complete list of all Penguin Readers titles, please contact your local Pearson Longman office or visit our website.

www.penguinreaders.com

Pirates of the Caribbean
The Curse of the Black Pearl

Elizabeth lives on a Caribbean island, a very dangerous place. A young blacksmith is interested in her, but pirates are interested too. Where do the pirates come from and what do they want? Is there really a curse on their ship? And why can't they enjoy their gold?

The Whistle and Dead Men's Eyes
M.R. James

Two Englishmen go away for a quiet holiday. But it is not very quiet in one man's hotel room. Somebody – or something – is using the other bed. What is it and why is it angry? The other man sees things, but they are not really there. Or are they? What is happening? *Read these ghost stories and be afraid. Be very afraid!*

Robinson Crusoe
Daniel Defoe

Robinson Crusoe is shipwrecked onto an island after a storm at sea. Are there other people? How will he survive? Will he be rescued? *A classic tale of survival based on a true story.*

There are hundreds of Penguin Readers to choose from – world classics, film adaptations, modern-day crime and adventure, short stories, biographies, American classics, non-fiction, plays ...

For a complete list of all Penguin Readers titles, please contact your local Pearson Longman office or visit our website.

Longman Dictionaries

Express yourself with confidence!

Longman has led the way in ELT dictionaries since 1935.
We constantly talk to students and teachers around the
world to find out what they need from a learner's dictionary.

Why choose a Longman dictionary?

Easy to understand

Longman invented the Defining Vocabulary – 2000 of the most common words which are used to write the definitions in our dictionaries. So Longman definitions are always clear and easy to understand.

Real, natural English

All Longman dictionaries contain natural examples taken from real-life that help explain the meaning of a word and show you how to use it in context.

Avoid common mistakes

Longman dictionaries are written specially for learners, and we make sure that you get all the help you need to avoid common mistakes. We analyse typical learners' mistakes and include notes on how to avoid them.

Innovative CD-ROMs

Longman are leaders in dictionary CD-ROM innovation. Did you know that a dictionary CD-ROM includes features to help improve your pronunciation, help you practice for exams and improve your writing skills?

**For details of all Longman dictionaries, and to choose
the one that's right for you, visit our website:**

www.longman.com/dictionaries